First World War
and Army of Occupation
War Diary
France, Belgium and Germany

74 (YEOMANRY) DIVISION
230 Infantry Brigade
Suffolk Regiment
15th Battalion
1 May 1918 - 24 June 1919

WO95/3153/3

Published by

The Naval & Military Press Ltd

Unit 10 Ridgewood Industrial Park,

Uckfield, East Sussex,

TN22 5QE England

Tel: +44 (0) 1825 749494

www.naval-military-press.com

www.nmarchive.com

This diary has been reprinted in facsimile from the original. Any imperfections are inevitably reproduced and the quality may fall short of modern type and cartographic standards.

© **Crown Copyright**
Images reproduced by permission of The National Archives, London, England, 2015.

Contents

Document type	Place/Title	Date From	Date To
Heading	WO95/3153/3 15 Battalion Suffolk Regiment		
Heading	74th Division 230th Infy Bde 15th Bn Suffolk Regt 1918 May-1919 Jun		
War Diary		01/05/1918	31/05/1918
War Diary	Penin	01/06/1918	17/06/1918
War Diary	Erny St Julien	01/07/1918	01/07/1918
War Diary	La Miquellerie	09/07/1918	09/07/1918
War Diary	Robecq Sector Bn HQ. at Carvin Farm	09/07/1918	17/07/1918
War Diary	Ham En Artois	17/07/1918	17/07/1918
Miscellaneous	Herewith War Diary Of 15th Suffolk	29/09/1918	29/09/1918
Miscellaneous	3rd Echelon	30/09/1918	30/09/1918
War Diary	Ham En Artois	01/08/1918	31/08/1918
War Diary	D.A.G 3rd Echelon B.E.F.	17/10/1918	17/10/1918
War Diary	Hind Leg Wood Reference Map France Sheet 62 1/40,000	01/09/1918	10/09/1918
War Diary	Templeux La Fosse Reference Sheet 62.c S.W. 1/20000	10/09/1918	30/09/1918
War Diary	Allouagne	01/10/1918	17/10/1918
War Diary	Arbrisseau	17/10/1918	17/10/1918
War Diary	Ronchin	18/10/1918	19/10/1918
War Diary	Baisieux Reference Map France Sheets 37 SE & SW 1/20000	20/10/1918	24/10/1918
War Diary	Marquain	25/10/1918	31/10/1918
War Diary	Haudion Reference Map Sheet 37 1/40000 And 37 SW 1/20000	01/11/1918	05/11/1918
War Diary	Malt House	06/11/1918	08/11/1918
War Diary	Hertain	08/11/1918	09/11/1918
War Diary	Tournai	10/11/1918	11/11/1918
War Diary	Dime	12/11/1918	12/11/1918
War Diary	Lahamaide Ref Sheet 38 1/40,000 (France & Belgium)	12/11/1918	17/11/1918
War Diary	Montroel Au Bois	17/11/1918	17/11/1918
War Diary	Mansart	18/11/1918	30/11/1918
War Diary	Mansart Reference Map France And Belgium Sheet 37 1/40,000	01/12/1918	06/12/1918
War Diary	Mansart	07/12/1918	14/12/1918
War Diary	Buissenal Ref Map Belgium Sheet 38 1/40,000	15/12/1918	16/12/1918
War Diary	Tournai 1/100,000	15/12/1918	16/12/1918
War Diary	Les Deux Acren	17/12/1918	17/12/1918
War Diary	Herinnes	18/12/1918	31/12/1918
War Diary	Herinnes Ref Map	01/01/1919	01/01/1919
War Diary	Belgium Sheet 38 1/40000	02/01/1919	02/01/1919
War Diary	Brussels 1/100,000	03/01/1919	06/01/1919
War Diary	Herinnes	07/01/1919	31/01/1919
Miscellaneous	Herewith War Diary For The Month of February 1919	01/03/1919	01/03/1919
War Diary	Herinnes Ref Map	01/02/1919	07/02/1919
War Diary	Belgium Sheet 38 1/40,000	01/02/1919	07/02/1919
War Diary	Brussels 1/100,000	07/02/1919	23/02/1919
War Diary	Herinnes	24/02/1919	24/02/1919
War Diary	Grammont	27/02/1919	01/04/1919
War Diary	Belgium (Ref Map Belgium Sheet 30 1/40,000)	01/04/1919	01/04/1919
War Diary	V.2.b.	04/02/1919	24/02/1919

War Diary	Grammont	25/04/1919	25/04/1919
War Diary	Belgium (ref Map Tournai 1/100,000)	04/05/1919	09/05/1919
War Diary	Grammont		
War Diary	Grammont	09/05/1919	31/05/1919
Miscellaneous	D.A.A.G. Passed	26/06/1919	26/06/1919
War Diary	Grammont Belgium (Ref Map Tournai 1/100,000 3.K.55 25)	05/06/1919	24/06/1919

WO/95/3153/3

15 Battalion Suffolk Regiment

74TH DIVISION
230TH INFY BDE

15TH BN SUFFOLK REGT

~~MAY DEC 1918~~
~~JAN JUN 1919~~

1918 MAY — 1919 JUN

Army Form C. 2118.

WAR DIARY
or
INTELLIGENCE SUMMARY
(Erase heading not required.)

230
B/74

15 Suffolk
vol 2

Place	Date	Hour	Summary of Events and Information	Remarks and references to Appendices
	14th May		Sailed from ALEXANDRIA. The voyage was uneventful for the first four days. On the morning of the 8th however a submarine was sighted, fired on with depth charges and believed to have been sunk.	
	7th		Landed in MARSEILLES & proceeded to Rest Camp, where he remained till the morning of the 9th when he entrained at MARSEILLES for NOYELLE.	
	12th		Reached NOYELLES about 1.30am. Went to staging camp for the rest of the night. About 9am he proceeded by 2½ march route to LAMOTTE-BULEUX.	
			While in this area the Bn was lectured to on the Spirit of the Bayonet by Lt Col CAMPBELL & on outrages committed by Huns.	
	15th		B.Ralph tk cape 9 & 0 officer Strength of Bn 36 Officers & 786 ORs.	1 2

WAR DIARY or INTELLIGENCE SUMMARY

Army Form C. 2118.

Place	Date	Hour	Summary of Events and Information	Remarks and references to Appendices
	May 21st		On the night of 21st the marched to RUE station and entrained there for a new billeting area. In this area the Bn was split up considerably. Bn HQ situated at HERLIN-LESEC with A & B coys. also stay at MAISNIL while C coy was divided between ECOCHE & TACHIN COURT.	
May	May 25th		Bn marched to PERIN where we remained. Trenches dug. Musketting carried on. Covenant all four companies being fairly closely situated. During the time considerable amount of training has been carried out. Good progress been made into Lewis Gunners and to the rifle shooting also bayonet fighting. Strength 37 officers 1777 ORs.	
	May 25th		Colonel & his four company commanders proceeded up lines trenches to the New Zealand Division to have a	

Army Form C. 2118.

WAR DIARY
or
INTELLIGENCE SUMMARY.
(Erase heading not required.)

Instructions regarding War Diaries and Intelligence Summaries are contained in F. S. Regs., Part II. and the Staff Manual respectively. Title pages will be prepared in manuscript.

Place	Date	Hour	Summary of Events and Information	Remarks and references to Appendices
Alto R	May 31		Alto R around. The strength of the Bn at this date was 36 Officers & 914 ORs. A. Rosling Capt & adjt. Suffolk Yeo Bn.	

WAR DIARY or INTELLIGENCE SUMMARY

15th Bn Suffolk R.
JUNE 1918
Army Form C. 2118.

Vol 3

Place	Date	Hour	Summary of Events and Information	Remarks and references to Appendices
PERIN	June 1st		Strength of Bn at this date was 39 officers 794 ORs. C.O. & Coy Commanders returned from tour round trenches with 1st ANZAC Division.	
	2nd		The Bn remained at PERIN until the 25th during which the two Bns attacked spent in training. There were several demonstrations of air-faith cooperation with Tanks & a Divisional Field Day.	
	12th		About this time the Division was kept on 9 hours notice instead of 24 hours. The state of readiness was raised frequently.	2
	14th		Lately CHO KB's have received strong new organisations each platoon has a strength of 3 Section (tactical) of 4 Lewis Gun sections each platoon. In other men, though 1 NCO & 10 men, the strain has proved too heavy, as the Platoon now left consists of 1 NCOs & 8 men each. No platoon has got its section strength near this	

WAR DIARY or INTELLIGENCE SUMMARY

Army Form C. 2118.

Place	Date	Hour	Summary of Events and Information	Remarks and references to Appendices
PERN	April 24th		Awaiting orders was received last night. Division would move next day. Early in the morning of the 24th orders were received that 75th would return to at LIGNY ST FLOCHEL at 10.10 a.m. He detrained the same day at AIRE & marched to ERNY ST JULIEN. Men along driving much but the Bn had considerable numbers of march casualties. By the Transport which were sent on first, by road spending a night on the road, & arriving at 12 noon the next day. On arrival he was kept at 4 hours notice to rejoin the XI & XIII Corps, & at 24 hours notice for the purpose of GHQ reserve. During the month a considerable amount of Xmas "Three day leave" occurred necessitating listening state. Cinemas & only open air concerts being allowed. During the month a few drafts were received	

WAR DIARY or INTELLIGENCE SUMMARY

Army Form C. 2118.

(Erase heading not required.)

Place	Date	Hour	Summary of Events and Information	Remarks and references to Appendices
			n/a 78k consisting of specialists amongst whom were 5 Signallers. Three hour Barrows.	
			Strength of M/Bn during month of June was as under.	
			June 8th AO OFF 899 ORs	
			15th 40 - 894	
			22nd 41 - 925	
			29 41 - 923	
1/7/18			R. Rolfe Cal. & rost for O.C.	
			15th (Norfolk) (Norway) Bn	
			Suffolk Regt	

Army Form C. 2118.

WAR DIARY
or
INTELLIGENCE SUMMARY.
(Erase heading not required.)

15th SUFFOLK YEO BN

July 1st – 31st inc.

Instructions regarding War Diaries and Intelligence Summaries are contained in F. S. Regs., Part II. and the Staff Manual respectively. Title pages will be prepared in manuscript.

Place	Date	Hour	Summary of Events and Information	Remarks and references to Appendices
ERNY ST JULIEN	July 1st		While in this village the Bn was kept at 4 hours notice both for preparing (in XI & XIII Corps area) SOS at 24 hours notice to prepare of CTR reserve. Reconnaissances were accordingly carried out of the ROBECQ line & (road) ST VENANT. During this time & a considerable amount of training was carried out, the facilities being good. There was an excellent range at BERGNY also a rifle range about 2 miles distant, where a lot of firing was done	
LA MIQUELLERIE	9th		The Bn left ERNY ST JULIEN to relieve the 61st Divn in the line before in trains to LA MIQUELLERIE & stopped for the night. On the night of 10th 11th 12th 12th the Bn was taken up as far as LABISETTE FARM in buses, thence they marched to the line, relieving the 2/5th Bn of the Norcolls in the right hand See for & relieved the	
ROBECQ SECTOR CALVIN FARM			the ROBECQ line & the Bn was in billets in ? Q & B Cops in the front line	2

WAR DIARY
or
INTELLIGENCE SUMMARY.
(Erase heading not required.)

Army Form C. 2118.

Place	Date	Hour	Summary of Events and Information	Remarks and references to Appendices
ROBECQ SECTOR BN HQ CARVIN FARM	17th		D Coy in the reserve line whilst A Coy was also in the rear, but in another line further back called the ANUSAIRE - HAVERSKERQUE line. After due consideration it was considered desirable to readjust the distribution, & only to hold the line very lightly with one or two in the reserve line. Accordingly on the night of 17/18 B Coy were withdrawn, being spreading out to the left while in Support spread to right the boundary being the ROBECQ - CALONNE road, & B Coy in this line took over part of the reserve line from the Support Spreading North of CALONNE road. This readjustment has carried out without casualties. The line was not in a good state of repair when taken over and a lot of work has been done which became at all events being up all night, which made the period one (needlessly) trying one although in other respects it was	

WAR DIARY or INTELLIGENCE SUMMARY

Army Form C. 2118.

Place	Date	Hour	Summary of Events and Information	Remarks and references to Appendices
ROBECQ SECTOR. BnHQ at CARVIN FARM.			Very quiet. Patrols were sent out every night, but have never encountered any of the enemy. The Boches seemed to rarely come out beyond his wire - owing to the standing crops it was so needful by ourselves to locate their patrols, if they had any out, so as to try & ambush them. There has been few casualties during the tenure of the 12 days this we were in the line - Major Hiss being killed & 4 wounded - one other death (that of HAWES of D Coy) was due to an accident - while working outside his trench the Shewyshmes fin with machine guns & Pt HAWES jumping back into the trench impaled himself on his bayonet. There has been practically no gas shelling, only one gas alarm being given, that in the neighbourhood of Bn HQ.
Battalion part of the 2nd/4th the Brigade was relieved by the 229 Bde, this unit being relieved by the 1/4th SOMERSETS - the relief was completed	

Place	Date	Hour	Summary of Events and Information	Remarks and references to Appendices
HAM EN ARTOIS			About 1am on the 26th the Bn marched by platoons to HAM-EN-ARTOIS. There were no casualties during the relief inspite of the fact that the enemy accorded a amount of shelling - for him most unusual. So that both the relief had somehow become known to the enemy. The Bn arrived in HAM EN ARTOIS about 3.30 am. on the morning of the 26th where he went into billets; our "B" teams had already arrived together things ready for us. Men here from two days rest knew to relax up their slates having again. Water supplies laid on to now quickly having better baths in the trenches then also order rum and brigade splendid. Lewis gunners were brushed up stood on a Bosch village. There observed bren slates. The facilities for training	

Army Form C. 2118.

WAR DIARY
or
INTELLIGENCE SUMMARY.
(Erase heading not required.)

Place	Date	Hour	Summary of Events and Information	Remarks and references to Appendices
HAM-EN-ARTOIS			Between known Units. While a Divisional reserve further reconnaissances were carried out forward (this) to look roads up the AMUSOIRES – HAVERSKERQUE line. The strength of the Bn. during this month were as under. July 6. 39 Officers 933 ORs. 13. 39 " 927 20. 39 " 943 27. 40 " 941 A Robus cabled to 4th for O.C. Suffolk Yorks Bn.	

Headquarters
74th (Yeo.) Division.   MLM   BMZ/19

Reference your AE/9, herewith War
Diary of 15th Suffolks for the month of
August 1918 which has been received only
today.

G Buxton
Lieut Colonel
Cmdg 230th Infantry Bde.

29/9/18.

R.B.9 A.E.9
34 October 1918 F

In continuation of this office No
A.E.9 of 17th instant, herewith War
Diary of O.C. 1st Bn Suffolk Regt
for month of August 1918.

30/9/18

H J Burchardt
Major General
Commanding 11th (too) Division

15 Suffolk R

WAR DIARY
or
INTELLIGENCE SUMMARY
(Erase heading not required.)

Army Form C. 2118.

230
/74 BEF

Place	Date	Hour	Summary of Events and Information	Remarks and references to Appendices
HAM EN ARTOIS	1/8/18		The Bn was still at HAM EN ARTOIS + having has carried out as much as possible. But on the 2nd morning orders were received that we would relieve the 231 Bde in the ST FLORIS sector. This unit in particular being 11th Brigade Reserve at HAMET BILLET.	
	4th		The Bn. marched off from 4am about 4.30 pm for days food sure from 1st Duke WELCH, without casualties.	
	5th		On the 5th ^ a warning order was received that the two front line Battalions were pushing forward their line in conjunction with the 239 Bde on our right that we were to be prepared to move at a moment's notice. Accordingly two coys were distributed in the M arnusoire -Thuverkerque line, & Bn HQ established at HOME FARM. Here we remained for two days entertaining officers + Bn HQ of the 230 Bde who would like to run the N.H.q	F 2

We received orders that the 230th Bd

WAR DIARY
or
INTELLIGENCE SUMMARY.
(Erase heading not required.)

Army Form C. 2118.

Place	Date	Hour	Summary of Events and Information	Remarks and references to Appendices
	16/6	16:00	Battalion on front & became ADVANCED GUARD Bn. This unit was to take over the front of the 209 Bde. Orders were that tos the Bn. marched from HOME FARM & after which the YIFE & FORFAR & SOMERSETS. The front line was along the TURBEAUTÉ.	
	16/6		Bn. moved after relief by 231st Bde. & positions in old RESERVE A.H. line that had been occupied for 8 days. Men chiefly were employed in moving the H.Q. line to & RAILWAY BRIGADE GULLY. About day of operations Vaily.	
			The 09/6 Bn. relief 231 Bde. in front line. Cols. Wilson, 1st 25 /R.W.F. & relieving 11—/32. On relief Bn. proceeded to BUSNES for two days when orders were received to return to ST HILAIRE - COTTES – to RIELLES when bivouacked W.II. The 29/6 when on the march to ST HILAIRE.	
	24:00		O/C. A/9 after journey arrived at JERRY when an advance ...)	

Army Form C. 2118.

WAR DIARY
or
INTELLIGENCE SUMMARY.
(Erase heading not required.)

Instructions regarding War Diaries and Intelligence Summaries are contained in F. S. Regs., Part II. and the Staff Manual respectively. Title pages will be prepared in manuscript.

Place	Date	Hour	Summary of Events and Information	Remarks and references to Appendices
	31		Advanced alongside Railway for two miles. On 16th of August 31st from Bray & proceeded to Mericourt. Relief of 16th 58th Division HQ. HQD LE a loon. Finishing HQ of 16th during Months later 29 inches. Strength. 3/8/18 43. 950 17/8/18 43 893 24/8/18 47 887 31/8/18 48 871	

A.E. 10.

D.A.G.
3rd Echelon B.E.F.
-------*-------

In continuation of this Office No. A.E. 10 of 15th and 17th instants, the following is forwarded in completion of War Diaries for month of September, 1918.

15th Battn. The Suffolk Regt.

19/10/18.

[signature]
Major General,
Commanding 74th (Yeomanry) Division.

74

15 Suffolk R

WS 6

Army Form C. 2118.

WAR DIARY
or
INTELLIGENCE SUMMARY.
(Erase heading not required.)

Instructions regarding War Diaries and Intelligence Summaries are contained in F. S. Regs., Part II. and the Staff Manual respectively. Title pages will be prepared in manuscript.

Place	Date	Hour	Summary of Events and Information	Remarks and references to Appendices
HIND LEG WOOD Reference map France Sheet 62. 1/40,000.	September 1.		The Bn remained hidden in vicinity of HIND LEG WOOD during the day. At 0230 on 2nd the Bn moved out in support of 229 Bde. In the evening the Bn manned SCUTARI TRENCH being in position about 1930.	
	3.		Remained in SCUTARI TRENCH still in support of 229 Bde.	
	4.	0830.	Two companies moved forward to relieve 12 Somersets (229 Bde) on line C.30 a.10.8. object of this movement was attack with 10th Buffs & the following morning in TEMPLEUX LA FOSSE — CURLU WOOD system of enemy trenches. South 231 Bde on right. The remainder of Bn was taken to Bn support to until during night B6. He Bn	
	5.	0930	the situation changed, on receipt of Bde orders No 61. The Bn was ordered to detail a Coy behind 231 Bde & take over from them the southern half of the divn front from E+W line through T.12.c.4. to the order Bn Boundary on E+W line through C.30.c.10.4. whole batch was to be kept with 10 Buffs.	
		11.30	The advance to pt W picotine (Blue line) was begun. The Bn formed up in rear of 231 Bde & pushed on. On approaching LARRIS French	
		1315	through the 231 Bde & pushed on. Bn experienced land net burst a muzzle very heavy shell fire was experienced.	
		1600	Barbed wire. Coming a good deal of confusion Trench (LARRIS) occupied & and advance continued on to YELLOW LINE W side of the line came under very heavy tank H & gun fire from	

WAR DIARY or INTELLIGENCE SUMMARY

Army Form C. 2118.

Place	Date	Hour	Summary of Events and Information	Remarks and references to Appendices
	September 5.	1900	from the right. Casualties a number of casualties in the leading Coys. Shelling HEAVY gas was also very heavy. The YELLOW line was not taken. The rocket went up and then exploded. Later lightly the C.O. decided to consolidate on the red and a short of yellow line + try + gain the north.	
	6.	0400	The advance was continued and yellow line occupied without opposition except from a few snipers.	
		0800	Shelling was continued against red line, which was occupied at 0900 with a few casualties.	
		1000	Advance continued and at 1200 it was reported that the Bn had reached the final objective. From personal reconnaissance the C.O. found that the right was still 300 yds behind. Orders were sent for the night to come up to the final objective on K.9. cuts. This was done soon after dark.	
	7.	0800	The 2.31 Bde passed through the Bn and the Bn was then concentrated in vicinity of K.2. The weather was very hot during the two days of advance + the country much cut up with old trenches and wire. Casualties approx: 100, including 2 coy commdrs + 3 other officers wounded. These casualties included gas casualties.	
	9-10.		Bn was in Bde Reserve in neighbourhood of TEMPLEUX LA FOSSE.	
	10.	1900	41e 230 Bde took over the line from 229 Bde.	

Army Form C. 2118.

WAR DIARY
or
INTELLIGENCE SUMMARY.
(Erase heading not required.)

Instructions regarding War Diaries and Intelligence Summaries are contained in F. S. Regs., Part II. and the Staff Manual respectively. Title pages will be prepared in manuscript.

Place	Date	Hour	Summary of Events and Information	Remarks and references to Appendices
TEMPLEUX LA FOSSE	Sept 10.	1900	Line now F.20.b.10.4. – F.19 cent – F.13 cent. M.Hx on right. 10th Buffs on left. 15th Suffolks in support. Moved off at 1900 and took over from 12th Donn. L.I. to Quiet night.	
Reference Sheet 62c SW 1/20000	11th		Reconnoitred forward to front line. Intermittent shelling during day, heavy from 1730 to 1930. Quiet night.	
	12/13		Remained in support	
	14		Bn took over front line from 16th Lancs & Australians on right	
	16/17		Remained in front line, nothing eventful happened	
	18.	12.30	Bn moved out to attack first objective, Green line L.4.7.1.0. – F.28.b.48. dispositions. B coy on right C coy on left. A and D in support respectively. Each coy two platoons out in two waves. Bn frontage 500 yds. TEMPLEUX LA GERARD was passed on left by assaulting coys & mopped up by D. Manoeuvre entirely successful, enemy surrender without much resistance, but M.Gs. were held out 'determinedly'. Dense fog. Attacks difficult to keep	
		07.31	1st Objective taken, and consolidation started	
		12 am	Fresh Bns passed through and Red line "was" was taken. D coy was moved up to new QUARRY, to support the Buffs. Bn H.Q. F.28.c.9.2.	
	19.		Quiet Day. Bn took over whole of Bde front from L.4. to S.Bde boundary.	
		28.25	move completed. Bn H.Q. F.27.b.3.6. During day much salvage was collected. Captures 18 MGs. 19 MGs. 300 prisoners. 30 M.Gs	
	20		Quiet day with intermittent shelling. More salvage collected. Bn moved	

WAR DIARY or INTELLIGENCE SUMMARY

Army Form C. 2118.

(Erase heading not required.)

Date	Hour	Summary of Events and Information	Remarks and references to Appendices
Sept 20		up after dark in support of 10th Buffs on R. and of others on left in attack on Blue line on following morning. Objective from A20.6.8.2 - A 14.C.4.3. Bn in position to follow B coy Rifleman Post. A coy Valley Post. C coy Tone Post. B coy TEMPLEUX South.	
21.	2100		
	0640	Green flare sent up indicating objective taken. Bn 413 F28.d.6.9.	
	0925	One platoon of D coy sent up to mop up 2 M.G. & 20 men in GUENNET trench.	
	0934	A coy sent up to support Buffs in - F.30.C.	
	1014	Buffs from Tone to send 1 coy to move to VALLEY Post, & 1 coy to TEMPLAR South. (B + C coys)	
	1030	2SRWF in Blue line	
	1130	Buffs asked for the platoons to mop up trenches in F.30. Sent from A coy	
	1300	Orders from Bde to send 1 coy to support Sx. at QUENNET COPSE.	
	1400	Front line troops were being driven back. Two coys moved up to support with R. Inniskillings (D coy) on R. Inniskillings L	
	4pm.	Orders received that Red line was to be held up to on R. Inniskillings L with R Hughlins on Rifleman Post.	
22.	2015	York now from Buffs to S. Div boundary. Throughout the day the shelling was very heavy, and the old trenches & shell holes gave casualties fortunately light. Heavy shelling during night. 1 killed 10 wounded.	
23. 25.		Regiment in front line. Heavy shelling at intervals. Bn relieved by Americans on night 24/25. Bn marched to	

Army Form C. 2118.

WAR DIARY
or
INTELLIGENCE SUMMARY.
(Erase heading not required.)

Place	Date	Hour	Summary of Events and Information	Remarks and references to Appendices
	Sept 25	1800	and entrained at 1500. Detrained at VILLERS BRETONNEAUX and marched to Billets in FOUILLY.	
	26 27	0800	marched to HERLIE and entrained. Day spent cleaning up and washing. Batts were available.	
	28	1500	Detrained at LILLERS and marched to Billets at ALLOUAGNE. Refitting, reorganising, cleaning up. Billets very comfortable	
	29.		do do	
	30		do do	
	31.		...ent orders received that the Bn. would relieve the 19th Div in line.	

Strength of Bn.
	Offrs	Others	
7/8		831	
14/8	41	734	effective
21/8	37	749	Strength
28/8	32		
	30.	721.	

Trench strength about 300 all ranks less than above figures.

AS Wood Lt for Adjt
15th (Suffolk Yeomanry) Bn
THE SUFFOLK REGIMENT

15th Suffolk Regt
OCM!

WAR DIARY
INTELLIGENCE SUMMARY.
(Erase heading not required)

Army Form C. 2118.

Sheet 36.A 1/40,000
Ref. Page (Sheet 36.S.W. & S.E. 1/20,000)

Place	Date October	Hour	Summary of Events and Information	Remarks and references to Appendices
ALLOUAGNE	1.	1000	The battalion had received orders to relieve the 19th Divs in the line in front of AUBERS. The Bn. marched and entrained on light Rly at CHOQUES	
		1200	detraining at LE TOURET carried out relief of the 2nd Wilts in daylight, taking over the line of resistance to 64 Ryle & it dusk the remaining two of 230 hole taking over front line	
		1900	Relief complete	
	2.		Quiet day with intermittent shelling. Bn remained in the line of resistance.	
	3.		The Bn moved up to old British front line by 1200 and remained in about line till 1900, when orders were received to move up to the AUBERS ridge line, so main line of resistance	
		2100	orders received that Bn. would take over from Buffs & Sussex	
	4.	0500	at 0800 on 4th and continue advance. The Bn moved out and passed through Buffs & Sussex, forming W line N+S line through V.8.b. Boundaries North E+W line through V8d 8.5.4; South E+W through V.20.a.8.5. Dispositions two coys in front line with two in support. 10KSLI on left Liverpool Scottish on right.	
		0915	First objective N+S line through V.10.b cent was reached without opposition	
		1030	Advance continued and halt was made on line N+S through	

WAR DIARY
INTELLIGENCE SUMMARY

Place	Date	Hour	Summary of Events and Information
	October 4.	11:15	V.12.a. One man wounded by shell fire. Touch was gained with K.S.L.I. but Bn on right could not get on, and line was consolidated covering the village of LATTRE and WAVRIN, with B, C and D Coys in the line, and A Coy in support. Bn HQ at V.8.c.5.3 with Advd Report Centre at V.10.d.8.7.
	5.	1300 to 16300	Heavy shelling. Patrols sent out and touch gained with enemy at various M.G. posts about 1000x in front. A light patrol met with considerable opposition from enemy M.G.s. Touch maintained with flanks. Daylight patrols, and Bn. O.P. in WAVRIN, located further enemy posts and Whippy Barg battery at V.23.c.3.5. Enemy movement observed along whole Bn front. Intermittent shelling throughout day. 3 men wounded on daylight patrol
	6.		Quiet day. Bn was relieved in the outpost line on the enemy by the 10th Buffs, 16 Sussex took over the line of resistance, and 13th Suffolks marched to billets in old Bosch hutments in woods surrounding FOURNES CHATEAU, with two Coys in W. end of SAINGHIN.
	7.		The day was spent in cleaning up and refitting. (plan HQ). Baths were available in WIERES and the two Coys billeted
	8.		in the woods were bathed. Proceeding on small parties to avoid enemy observation. The two Coys in SAINGHIN were unable to

WAR DIARY or INTELLIGENCE SUMMARY

Army Form C. 2118.

Place	Date	Hour	Summary of Events and Information	Remarks and references to Appendices
	October			
	9.		Also observation to move. One coy from the wood was sent to dig a company redoubt on a new line of resistance, posts of redoubt being sighted during day. A new line of resistance was being dug as the Bde had orders supplied about 300 yds. North the 155th taking over our next previous posts. Huts in wood heavily shelled during night. One civilian killed & one wounded. Orders received that Bn would take over new outpost line towards FOURNES on night 10/11th and dig a series of coy redoubts of resistance.	
	10.		This line was sighted during day in conjunction with Bde HQ. The posts commenced on the night of the 8th forming part of the line. One coy was sent at dusk to complete this post. Bn marched by coys at dusk to positions of selected redoubts and the new line of resistance was dug during night.	
	11.		Quiet day. A few small shells fell on and about new posts. Weather was bad, and a certain amount of R.E. material was sent up at night with rations, for protecting & improving posts.	
	12. 13.		Bn remained in this line with Bn. HQ in FOURNES. Orders received that Bn would take over front line on night 13/14th, relieving the 16th Sussex.	
	13		Bn relief was carried out by 11.0, but was rather hindered as during	

WAR DIARY or INTELLIGENCE SUMMARY.

Army Form C. 2118.

4

Place	Date October	Hour	Summary of Events and Information	Remarks and references to Appendices
	14.		the day, the Knosse had advanced their posts some 600 yds. Bn. HQ at in Boche huts at CHATEAU DE LA VALLÉE. Active patrolling, and enemy was found in strength all along front. 2/Lt A.M. CROWTHER and his runner were killed during night, being buried by a shell.	
	15.		Daylight patrols found enemy still occupying posts in front, as he was suspected of withdrawing. Enemy retired slowly during night. The fact was first discovered by an offr of organized raiding party, finding L.A.HAIE & field forts empty. The Bn moved on to 9am touch forthwith.	
	16.	0500	On reaching the canal HAUTE DEULE strong opposition was met & Bn withdrew to positions covering SANTES & ROSOIR about 1000 yds W of canal. Orders received to continue advance and push on over canal. Casualties on 16th 4 killed and 7 wounded. LT. J.J. HENDERSON afterwards	
	17.	0600	Advanced made with two coys in front and two in support of wounded Right Coy in conjunction with R.E. went over canal by 0830. Enemy retired offering no resistance. All coys over by 0930, croft bridges being erected. Advanced continued and final objective Rly line between WATTIGNIES & FACHES reached by 1500. 10th Buff went through at 1800, and 231 Bde relieved 230 Bde during night.	
ARBISSEAU		2200	Bn went into billets in ARBISSEAU	

Army Form C. 2118.

WAR DIARY
or
INTELLIGENCE SUMMARY.
(Erase heading not required.)

Place	Date	Hour	Summary of Events and Information	Remarks and references to Appendices
RONCHIN	18		Bn. moved from ABBISSEAU to RONCHIN, and was settled in billets by 1500. Pickets were posted at night to each end of village.	
	19.		Day spent in cleaning up, moved to AUSTAIGN at 2000 and billeted there.	
BAISIEUX Reference map FRANCE SHEETS 37 SE & SW 1/20000	20	0100	Orders received to move at 0800 on 20th to billet in BAISIEUX. Bn. billeted in BAISIEUX by 1200. Pickets placed on exits of village.	
	21.	0845.	Fire suddenly broke out in a large house occupied by B & C Coy's, the whole building being enveloped in flames in a few minutes. Investigation proved the cause was from stove delayed action fuses. 3 killed & 5 injured, all equipment & much clothing destroyed; as a foot & kit inspection was in progress at the time.	
BAISIEUX	22.		Day spent in training under company arrangements, refitting 2 coy's which had lost Kit in fire. Orders from Bde to withdraw pickets. Warning order received that 230th Bde would relieve 229 Bde on night 23/24th	
do.	23	0600	on line on night 23/24th C.O. & O.C. coys proceeded to trace with opposite number (16th Devons) prior to relief.	
		1300	Relief cancelled.	
		1600	Relief ordered to take place on night 24/25th	

Army Form C. 2118.

WAR DIARY
or
INTELLIGENCE SUMMARY.
(Erase heading not required.)

Instructions regarding War Diaries and Intelligence Summaries are contained in F. S. Regs., Part II. and the Staff Manual respectively. Title pages will be prepared in manuscript.

Place	Date	Hour	Summary of Events and Information	Remarks and references to Appendices
BAISIEUX	24		Coy training in morning. 'B' teams sent up to Transport lines from our Reception Camp. 35 o.r.s returned from hospital. Please	
		1730	Marched out to relieve Devons in reserve at MARQUAIN. 11th Division in support. 10th Buffs in line (front) about O.14.d - O.21.a to O.27.d.	
MARQUAIN	25/26		Bn. remained in support in billets and carried on with certain amount of training in Lewis gun drill. Movement kept a minimum as village was only about 2000 yds from front line.	
	27		A & D coys detailed to man outpost line of resistance, O.25.d.20 to O.25.b.3.4. (A coy) and O.25.b.3.4. to O.19.cent. (D coy). B & C coys counter-attack coys in MARQUAIN. The above line was dug during night, forward to 4 platoon posts to coy HQ per coy. A & D coys battalion to hills at Thephina.	
	27 →		B & C coys manned outpost line of resistance at night & improved posts. A & D coys remained in billets. Orders received that 2 coys of 15 Suffolks & 2 coys 11th Devons would relieve 10th Buffs in front line on night 28/29. Remaining coys	
	28	2100	manning outpost line of resistance. Relief complete & patrols out during night having holding line strongly. M.G's active. 55 Bn.d on right 16 howrs on left about 100 G.S. & H.E. shells fell in MARQUAIN during night, mostly targets were batteries there, but several shells fell round Bn. HQ	
	29	0100 0200		
			well. S.B.R's were worn for about an hour.	

Army Form C. 2118.

WAR DIARY
or
INTELLIGENCE SUMMARY.
(Erase heading not required.)

Place	Date	Hour	Summary of Events and Information	Remarks and references to Appendices
MARQUAIN	29.		Quiet day in line. Intermittent gas shelling on front & support lines. Warning order received that 230th Bde would be relieved by 231st Bde on night 30/31st; 230th Bde taking over duties of picquetting the town TOURNAI when taken; and also the responsibility of manning the main line of Resistance running N.35.b - N.29.a. - N.29.a. - N.23.c - N.23.b - N.17.d.	
	30.		Quiet day in line, patrols of previous night found enemy still occupying posts strongly, enemy shelled intermittently during day with gas + H.E. 15th Suffolks were relieved by 10th K.S.L.I. branches from 2.5ᵃ - 3.0ᵃ 3 O.R. wounded. Relief complete, Bns marching independently to billets allotted in HAUDION. Bn HQ at N.28.d.7.1.	
	31.	2/1/5	Morning was spent in foot, kit and general inspections. Bde commdrs conference at Bde HQ to discuss TOURNAI picquets, and manning of eastern exits of TOURNAI from 0.23.a.6.0 - 0.30.b.1.9 and resistance. The Bn was detailed to picquet the eastern exits of TOURNAI from 0.23.a.6.0 - 0.30.b.1.9 with guards on various bridges. The Bn had to be prepared to ⎯⎯ held main line of resistance from N.35.a.9-5. to N.23.c.9.1., with two coy in line and two in support.	
			Casualties for October:- K. W. M.	
			Officers - 1 1 (had of wounds) 5* signed (from prev 21ˢᵗ)	
			O.Rs - 11 11 4 5* (*1 since died of wounds)	

WAR DIARY
or
INTELLIGENCE SUMMARY.

(Erase heading not required.)

Army Form C. 2118.

Summary of Events and Information

Effective Strength of Bn. during October.

5th Oct. — 30 offrs — 716 ors.
12th " — 34 " — 717 "
19th " — 34 " — 715 "
26th " — 33 " — 694 "

The w/m were awarded the M.M. for the SERRE operations during Sept.

45860 Pte W.R. Parker
9047 " L. Brown
320746 A/C/ J. Rignell
320609 Pte R. Day
240723 — A.E. Grove
320657 — H.C. Harvey
50616 — F. Ioleland.

H.P.Wood Lt. a/adjt
for Lieut Colonel
Commanding 1st (North Yorkshire) Bn
THE SUFFOLK REGIMENT

Army Form C. 2118.

WAR DIARY or INTELLIGENCE SUMMARY.

(Erase heading not required.)

15th (Ser Bn.) Suffolk Regt

Place	Date November	Hour	Summary of Events and Information	Remarks and references to Appendices
HAUDION Reference Map Sheet 37. 1/40,000 and 37.SW. 1/20,000	1		Coy training and specialist in billeting area. Platoon commanders to shew that platoons for at least one hour in the morning and one hour in the afternoon. # One O.R. killed during night from hostile shelling	
		1500	Warning order received that an operation was taking place on the Divn (front at daybreak on 2nd inst. Bn ordered to be ready to move with Transport at two hours notice B & C Coys improved posts of main line of resistance (during night) which ran N.35.b — N.29.c — N.29.a — N.23.c	
	2	0900	No development from operation and no orders from Bde the Bn carried on with normal work for rest of day. A & D Coys worked for 3 hours during the night on posts of main line of resistance	
	3	0930	Voluntary church service in selected billet. (A. & D.)	
		1300 to 1700	Three companies and Bn. HQ sent to the baths at BAISIEUX An order received during the afternoon that the B.g.C. would inspect the Bn and Transport at 1000 on 6th inst.	
	4	1000	A Bn parade to practice march past etc for inspection "C" Coy used the baths at BAISIEUX during the afternoon. Remaining troops at disposal of Coy commanders. B'way continued work on night front by posts at night.	
	5		Very wet day training confined to billets. Orders received that Bn would move and billet in MALT HOUSE (M.18.C.) on 6th	
MALT HOUSE	6	1200	Wet day. Bn marched out at 0930 and was settled in billets in MALT HOUSE about midday.	

Army Form C. 2118.

WAR DIARY
or
INTELLIGENCE SUMMARY.
(Erase heading not required.)

Instructions regarding War Diaries and Intelligence
Summaries are contained in F. S. Regs., Part II.
and the Staff Manual respectively. Title pages
will be prepared in manuscript.

Place	Date	Hour	Summary of Events and Information	Remarks and references to Appendices
MALT HOUSE.	7		Orders received that B.G.C's inspection cancelled by now ob/n would now take place on 8th. The Bn was engaged in cleaning up generally.	
	8	0800	C.O. inspected boys in full marching order in afternoon. Orders received to move at 0900 and take over duties of picqueting the eastern exit of TOURNAI in accordance with instructions issued and taken over on relief of 30/31st Bns, when 230th Bde became the 'TOURNAI Brigade'.	
		0900	Bn marched out at 0900 complete with all transport.	
		1000	Orders received from Bde that TOURNAI was not yet cleared of enemy. Bn ordered to billet in HERTAIN (N.21.)	
HERTAIN.		1200	Bn billetted in HERTAIN	
		2000	Orders received that Bn would march out at 0800 and take over pickets from 24th Welsh on eastern exits of TOURNAI from 0.23.a.6.0. – 0.30.b.1.9. 16th Sussex picketed southern exits and 10th Buffs western exits. All exits & entrances to town were sealed & no soldiers or civilians could pass unless in possession of a special pass.	
	9.	0800	Bn marched out.	
		1500.	Relief of 24th Welsh complete. Bn. H.Q. at 0.24.d.0.7.	
TOURNAI.	10.		Picqueting TOURNAI. Orders received that Bn would be relieved by 18th Londons at 07.30 on 11th.	
	11.	0900	Relieved by 18th Londons.	
		0915	Wire from Bde stated that hostilities would cease at 1100. Bn to stand fast.	

Army Form C. 2118.

WAR DIARY
or
INTELLIGENCE SUMMARY.

(Erase heading not required.)

Instructions regarding War Diaries and Intelligence Summaries are contained in F. S. Regs., Part II. and the Staff Manual respectively. Title pages will be prepared in manuscript.

Place	Date	Hour	Summary of Events and Information	Remarks and references to Appendices
D:M.E	11.	11/15	Orders received that the 230th Bde Group would march Eastwards. Billeting parties sent forward to meet Staff Capt. to arrange billets.	
	12	1600.	Bn settled in billets in L.25. and 26.	
		0500	Orders received that Bn would march further Eastwards and billet in LAHAMAIDE. Bn to pass Bde starting point at L.27.b.7.7. at 1000.	
LAHAMAIDE	12.	1330	Bn arrived at new billets. Orders were received that the Bn would be employed on roads and ditches.	
M/Sheet 38. 1/40.000. (France & Belgium)	13.		A & B Coys employed on road in morning, C & D in afternoon. These companies were employed in cleaning equipment and washing vehicles in morning.	
	14		Work on roads continued. Warning order received that D.Q.C. would inspect the Bn on afternoon 15th. in marching Bn to march past as per document.	
	15		Morning spent in cleaning up and drill.	
		1430	D.Q.C's inspection and afterwards presented M.M. to the following who gained them for their actions on the SOMME on Sept. last. 320.402.L/Sgt SMITH.J.C. 320609 Pte DAY.R. 320612. Pte HOUGH.F. 9047 Cpl BROWN.L. 5061b — CLELAND.F.	
	16.	0900	Bn marched out, with Bde Group, about 8 miles west for work on the TOURNAI — LEUZE Railway. Bn was billeted for two nights in MONTROEVL AUX BOIS and BARBERE	
	17.			

WAR DIARY
or
INTELLIGENCE SUMMARY.

Army Form C. 2118.

Place	Date	Hour	Summary of Events and Information	Remarks and references to Appendices
MONTROEUIL AU BOIS	17.		Church parade was held in the village church a special service was held, a thanksgiving service for the cessation of hostilities.	
	18.	0930.	Bn. marched out and proceeded to MANSART. (Q.35.) where it was billeted. Bn HQ in CHATEAU.	
MANSART.	19.		Work was commenced on Railway, which had been blown up every few yards by the Boche, with a considerable number of large mine craters. Work was carried out under supervision of 5th Bn. Canadian R.E. Two companies worked in morning and two in the afternoon. Hours of work 0830 to 1200 and 1200 to 1530. Information was received that the B.de would probably remain in this area for 3 or 4 weeks. Work on Rly continued. A & B coys received 1st dose of T.A.B. in the evening.	
	20		Railway work continued. 10 ot per coy attended at lecture at TOURPIN. by Sir. F. Younghusband. C & D coys received 1st dose of T.A.B.	
	21.		Railway work. do. Boche baths in the village had been repaired	
	22.		do. A & B coys used baths in afternoon.	
	23.		do.	
	24. (Sunday.)		do.	
	25		Coys carried out training (close order drill and Guard duties) for the period of the day they were not at work.	

WAR DIARY or INTELLIGENCE SUMMARY

Army Form C. 2118.

Place	Date	Hour	Summary of Events and Information	Remarks and references to Appendices
MAUBEUGE	26	14.00	Work on Railway continued. Lecture by G.S.O.2 on demobilisation and Education Scheme, for all Officers and N.C.Os and selected privates.	
	27		Work on Railway. C&D Company were bathed during the day and B Company received the 2nd dose of inoculation in the evening.	
	28		Railway work continued by C&D Coys.	
	29		" " " " " " The Foden lorry (for disinfection) was available for the battalion. All clothing and blankets were disinfected during the day. C&D Coys received 2nd dose of inoculation in the evening.	
	30		A&B Coys at work on Railway. The W/m have received the following awards (during the month) as shown opposite their names:— Capt/Major A/Lt Col. T. de la G. Grissell. awarded M.C. 320961. Sgt. E.H. Kingsley " D.C.M. 200.231. W. BEADON " D.C.M. 320.178 J. MACPHERSON " M.M. Strength of Bn:— Officers ORs 2nd Mar 33 693 9th 29 666 16th 30 700 23rd 31 719 30th 37 765.	Admitted Hospital sick during month Officers 2 ORs 109 mostly suffering from influenza. 25% of these have rejoined.

H.P. Wood Lt
Lieut Colonel
Commanding 15th (Suffolk Yeomanry) Bn
THE SUFFOLK REGIMENT

WAR DIARY
or
INTELLIGENCE SUMMARY.
(Erase heading not required.)

Army Form C. 2118.

15th Bn Suffolk Regt.

Instructions regarding War Diaries and Intelligence Summaries are contained in F. S. Regs., Part II. and the Staff Manual respectively. Title pages will be prepared in manuscript.

Summary of Events and Information 15th Ser. Bn. Suffolk Regt.

Place	Date	Hour	Summary of Events and Information	Remarks and references to Appendices
MANSt. RT. Refrce. FRANCE & BELGIUM Sheet 37. 1/40,000	December 1 (Monday)		A & B Companies continued work on the TOURNAI - LEUZE Rly. C & D Companies ceased work owing to insulation on the evening of 29th ult.	
	2.		No work. The day being wet and made for recreational training. A cross country run, consisting of a team of 6 all ranks from each coy and Bn. Hq., was run off during the morning. Distance 2-3 miles. On Hq. team were each awarded later platoon & Company football matches were played off throughout the day. The Divisional Band.	
	3.		No great. played selections from 1400 to 1600 at Bn. Hq. All companies employed on Railway. C & D in the morning being relieved by A & B in the afternoon. The Men used the divisional Baths throughout the day. There was a complete change of clothing per man. See note.	
	4.		Wet day. A & B coys on Railway in morning and C & D coys in the afternoon. Companies not working in the afternoon, played off their football matches. Companies not working in the morning, at disposal of coy commanders. Warning orders received from D.H.Q. that the M.P.M. the King would probably pass through the area on the 11th inst. and that the rifles would later be served out and details to follow later.	
	5.		Work on Rly. as previous day.	
	6.		do.	

WAR DIARY
or
INTELLIGENCE SUMMARY.

Army Form C. 2118.

(Erase heading not required.)

Instructions regarding War Diaries and Intelligence Summaries are contained in F. S. Regs., Part II. and the Staff Manual respectively. Title pages will be prepared in manuscript.

Place	Date	Hour	Summary of Events and Information	Remarks and references to Appendices
MANSART.	December 7.		H.M. the King visited the III Corps on his way from Brussels to Tournai. The 14th Yeo Division was drawn up in either side of the main LEUZE-TOURNAI road just west of MANSART. The King arrived about 12.00, descended from his Car and proceeded on foot alongside the road, on which the men of the division arranged 8 or 9 ranks on either side. His Majesty had a great reception.	
	8.		Sunday. No railway work. The day was set aside for recreation. Inter battalion + company football matches were played off.	
	9		Work on Railway continued. C&D companies for the morning period, being relieved by M&B for the afternoon. Took work as always but when possible.	
	10.		A+B coys on Railway in the morning, C+D in the afternoon. Bn HQ used the baths in the afternoon, clean underclothing available.	
	11.		Work on Railway. C+D coy in the morning, A+B in the afternoon. The 4 coys used the baths during the day, at times allotted when they were not working.	
	12 13		Work on Railway. Rain fell off + on during these days. Warning orders received that the Bn would move to HERINNES (F.8.a. sheet 38 1/40,000), starting on the 13th making 3 days march. Advanced billeting parties proceed by bus to new area at 08.00 on 13th.	

Army Form C. 2118.

WAR DIARY
or
INTELLIGENCE SUMMARY.
(Erase heading not required.)

Instructions regarding War Diaries and Intelligence Summaries are contained in F. S. Regs., Part II. and the Staff Manual respectively. Title pages will be prepared in manuscript.

Place	Date	Hour	Summary of Events and Information	Remarks and references to Appendices
MANSART	December 14		Work on Railway. Bn orders no 86 received with detailed orders for the first days march. Extra transport consisting of two motor lorries were allotted to each Coy to carry blankets and Xmas stores.	
BUISSENAL ref map BELGIUM sheet 38. 1/40,000 and TOURNAI 1/100,000	15.	0900	The Bn marched out and arrived at BUISSENAL about 1300 and billeted for the night. The next march was to be a brigade march and the Bn received orders to billet in LES DEUX ACREN.	
	16.	0830	The Bn marched from billets at BUISSENAL and joined the head of the Brigade column at G.3.a.8.3. The length of the march today was from 21.6.22 kilometers and it was an unpleasant wet day. The Bn arrived at LES DEUX ACREN at 1400, and billeted E. of river.	
LES DEUX ACREN	17.	0900	The Bn marched out from billets for final destination, arriving at HERINNES about 1230. The billets on the whole were good, but without a few suitable halls for education and indoor recreation, but without eating accommodation, which seating was indented for on the R.E.	
HERINNES	18		This day was spent in a general clean up of equipment and clothing, which suffered from the previous three days march, in the continual wet and mud.	
	19		Company training from 0900 to 1100, which included a thorough inspection of companies by their company commanders. The	

Army Form C. 2118.

WAR DIARY
or
INTELLIGENCE SUMMARY.
(Erase heading not required.)

Instructions regarding War Diaries and Intelligence Summaries are contained in F. S. Regs., Part II. and the Staff Manual respectively. Title pages will be prepared in manuscript.

Place	Date	Hour	Summary of Events and Information	Remarks and references to Appendices
HERINNES	December 19 20		Inter-platoon football competition was started in the afternoon. Company training from 0900 to 1100 which included guard and sentry drill, and saluting. The inter-platoon football competition was continued in the afternoon. Bn HQ was reckoned as a company of 4 platoons for this competition.	
	21		Programme of work as for previous day. Elementary Educational training was started, classes were held from 1000 -1200 in the local school, accommodation for about 50 persons.	
	22 Sunday		Church parade at 0930 in Cinema Hall. Continuation of inter-platoon football competition in afternoon.	
	23		Orders were received that the priority of training would be as follows Education, Recreation, Military. The day to be divided amongst these forms of training approximately. 0900 to 1000 Military training 1300 to 1600 Recreational training 1000 to 1200 Educational do 1700 to 2000 Educational and indoor-recreational training The C.O. inspected "A" Company at 0900 Remaining companies under company arrangements, to include section & platoon drill.	
	24.	0900 to 1200	Bn route march. The military training had to include two route marches per week. Parades to be as strong as possible including cooks, grooms etc. and transport.	

WAR DIARY
or
INTELLIGENCE SUMMARY.
(Erase heading not required.)

Army Form C. 2118.

Place	Date	Hour	Summary of Events and Information	Remarks and references to Appendices
HERINNES	25.		Christmas Day, no training. Rugby football match was arranged between the Officers and Sergts. Officers won 12 - 9.	
	26.		Boxing Day, no military training. Paper chase in morning. Continuation of Company football league in the afternoon.	
	27.		Inspection of 'B' Coy by C.O. at 0900. Platoon Drill and Bayonet fighting. Education, general, from 0900 to 1200. Latter Platoon football competition continued in afternoon.	
	28.		Very wet day. Route march not ordered, was cancelled. Lectures by officers to companies. Coy football league in afternoon. Bde. H.Q. v A. Coy. A. Coy won 2 - 1. The Divisional Cinema arrived, for showing on 28 & 29th. The Cinema Hall of the village provided excellent accommodation.	
	29.		Sunday. Church parade in Cinema Hall at 1000. 2 Coy Coy football league continued in afternoon. Cinema show 1700 - 1900.	
	30.		C.O. inspected C. Coy from 0900 to 1000. Remaining Coy's physical drill platoon & company drill. Lewis gun & musketry subjects to known from 1000 to 1130. from with exception of those who went to the cinema. Later. Platoon football in afternoon.	
	31.		C.O. inspected D. Coy. 0900 to 1000. Remaining companies as for previous day. Coy League football in afternoon. B. Coy v. Bde. H.Q. 3 - 0. result of draw. Since arriving at HERINNES rain has fallen on every day except Xmas day.	

Army Form C. 2118.

WAR DIARY
or
INTELLIGENCE SUMMARY.
(Erase heading not required.)

Instructions regarding War Diaries and Intelligence Summaries are contained in F. S. Regs., Part II. and the Staff Manual respectively. Title pages will be prepared in manuscript.

Place	Date	Hour	Summary of Events and Information	Remarks and references to Appendices
HERINNES	December		Strengths at intervals during the month	

            Effective   Fighting
      OFFRS   ORs   OFFRS   ORs
Dec. 6th — 37 — 756   30 — 664
13th — 38 — 753   31 — 695
20th — 39 — 758   31 — 707
27th — 39 — 755   28 — 705

Admitted each during the month 10 officers and 55 O.R.

Extract London Gazette 24th Aug 18. Mentons. Suffolk Yeomanry T.F.
Gunners Lt. Col. the Hon. W.E. D.S.O.
Jarvis Lt. Col. F.W.
Langley 2/Lt. P. (attd 15th yeo on Suffolk Regt)

F.W. Wood Capt
a/adjutant Lieut. Colonel
Commanding 15th (Suffolk Yeomanry) Bn
THE SUFFOLK REGIMENT

WAR DIARY
or
INTELLIGENCE SUMMARY

(Erase heading not required.) 15th Suffolk Yeo: Bn Suffolk Regt.

Army Form C. 2118.

Place	Date	Hour	Summary of Events and Information	Remarks and references to Appendices
HERINNES ref map BELGIUM Sheet 38 1/40000. and BRUSSELS 1/100,000.	January 1919. 1		New Year's Day was observed as a holiday for the Division. No guards were to be mounted, unless absolutely necessary, between 1600 on 31st Dec 18 to 0900 on 2nd Jan 19. Football competition were continued with in the afternoon.	
	2.		Military training of 1st ½ hr daily consisted of toy drill and training of specialists. Educational training from 0900 – 1200 in general subjects and from 1400 to 1600 in special subjects. Recreation in the afternoon. 'B' Coy V 'C' Coy in the Bde adjt/league, result a draw. A pick up team play the Royal Monmouth R.E.'s are rugger, result 10-6.	
	3.		Training as for previous day. Company football league continued in afternoon. A battalion concert party had been reorganised and gave its first show this evening.	
	4.		A Relation Route march from 0900 to 1100, about 10 to 11 kilos distance. 'A' Coy played Bde HQ in Coy league. Bde HQ won (1-0). Some organised boxing bouts were fought off. Some good spirited bouts were witnessed. Prizes were given to the winners of weights.	
	5.		Sunday, Church parade at 0930.	
	6.		Military training (including coy drill) Educational training as for previous days programme. Bde Coy league football in afternoon.	

92

Army Form C. 2118.

WAR DIARY
or
INTELLIGENCE SUMMARY.

(Erase heading not required.) 15th Suffolk Geo. Bn. Suffolk Regt.

Place	Date	Hour	Summary of Events and Information	Remarks and references to Appendices
HERINNES	January 7		No more military training under coy. arrangements, Education and Recreation as for previous day.	
	8.		Bn. Route March from 0900 to 1100. Orders issued from Brigade that future route marches could be made in drill order, instead of marching order. All animals on the strength of the Bn. were inspected & classified by a Veterinary Board. The Bn. football team played the 25.R.W.F. at CRAMMONT. result Bn. won 3-0.	
	9.		Coy. drill 0900-1100 including 2 hrs. bayonet fighting. Education as usual. Specialist The C.O. lectured to N.C. Coy's & Bn. H.Q. subject "Problems of Demobilisation". Inter-platoon football in afternoon. Dance for O.R.'s & civilians at 1900. 1 Officer (Capt. D.B. Green) & 5 O.R.'s demobilised.	
	10.		Military training & Education as for previous day. C.O. lectured to B & D Coy's & Bn. H.Q. subject as for previous day. In future company officers to lecture daily for av. hr. between 1100 & 1200, on the leading daily topics. Leading articles from newspapers on demobilisation, reconstruction etc. could be used out as an alternative to lectures. Leave for O.R's to U.K. cancelled owing to increase in numbers for demobilisation.	
	11.		Military training & Education as for previous day. Inter-platoon football in afternoon. 22 O.R's demobilised.	
	12.		Church parade at 9.30. Inter-platoon football in afternoon.	
	13.		O.R's demobilised.	

Army Form C. 2118.

WAR DIARY
or
INTELLIGENCE SUMMARY.

(Erase heading not required.) 15th Yeo. Bn: Suffolk Regt.

Instructions regarding War Diaries and Intelligence Summaries are contained in F.S. Regs., Part II. and the Staff Manual respectively. Title pages will be prepared in manuscript.

Place	Date	Hour	Summary of Events and Information	Remarks and references to Appendices
HERINNES	January 13.		Military training & Education as previously. A Thos schoolroom previously used as a billet was vacated & prepared for Education (i.e. special subjects Book-keeping). Inter platoon football in afternoon.	
	14.		Military training 0900–1000. Education 0900–1200 general, 1200–1400 to 1600 Special subjects. Inter League football D. Coy v. Bn.HQ. Result Bn.HQ won 3–1. 14 ord. demobilized.	
	15.		Morning programme as for previous day. Inter league football at 1400 A Coy v B Coy. 10 officers and 24 ors demobilized (2/Lt H.T FOSTER). 1400 to 1600 Special subjects. Inter football team played the	
	16.		Morning programme as per 14th inst. An football team. Bn. from 2–1. 16 heroes (Army Cup) at GRAMMONT in the afternoon. On arrival (to shew to the Bn.) on pint concert party and band arrived. The local cinema hall fitted with a stage & electric light, and accommodation for about 500 persons made a very convenient hall.	
	17.		Military training and education as previously. Inter platoon football in afternoon.	
	18.		Training as for previous day. Continuation of Coy. & give football 'C' Coy v 10 del HQ. 10 del HQ. won 1–0. in afternoon. 14 ors demobilized.	
	20 Sunday		Church parade in cinema Hall at 0930. 1 officer 2/Lt B.A. Postgray and 29 ors demobilized	

Army Form C. 2118.

WAR DIARY
or
INTELLIGENCE SUMMARY.
(Erase heading not required.)   15th Yeo Bn Suffolk Regt.

Place	Date	Hour	Summary of Events and Information	Remarks and references to Appendices
HERINNES	January 1919 20.		The Bn was ordered to find a company of 5 officers and 175 O.Rs to be attached to the 10th Buffs for the Review by the King of Belgium on the 26th instant. Men were selected from all Coys. Remainder of Bn under company arrangements for Military Training. 2 Ex Platoon Football were held in the afternoon. Special parade was inspected by the B.G.C. Brussels Brigade. Bn moved	
	21 to 28		On 22nd and 24th they were inspected by the B.G.C. Brussels Brigade. Bn moved on morning of the 25th. This company was entrained at HERINNES & proceeded to BRUSSELS where arrangements for billeting etc, in conjunction with 10th Buffs, had been made. This company returned on the 28th. From the 22nd to 28th the remainder of the Bn. continued training under company arrangements, strength of coys were weakened by absence of Brussels Coy; Education classes were reduced, but general education was carried on, & only special subjects omitted. 6 O.Rs demobilized on 21st " 22nd 5 " 24th 5 " 26th 3 "	
	29.-31		The weather had been frosty recently, snow fell on the 26th & this hard weather has prevented all games, snow 22 & snow. Hard frosty weather prevailed. Military Training daily carried	

Army Form C. 2118.

WAR DIARY
or
INTELLIGENCE SUMMARY.

(Erase heading not required.) 15th Geo. Bn. Suffolk Regt.

Instructions regarding War Diaries and Intelligence Summaries are contained in F. S. Regs., Part II. and the Staff Manual respectively. Title pages will be prepared in manuscript.

Place	Date	Hour	Summary of Events and Information	Remarks and references to Appendices
HERINNES	29/1/31.		of physical training and close order drill. Education in general and special subjects at usual times. FODEN LORRY arrived on evening of 30th for disinfecting blankets. 'D' + 'C' Coys blankets were done on the 31st. Strength of Bn. at intervals during month:-	
			Effective Strength Ration Strength	
			OFFRS ORS OFFRS ORS	
			Jan:	
			3rd 39 — 762 24 — 699	
			10th 37 — 736 22 — 679	
			17th 36 — 682 20 — 619	
			24th 34 — 617 18 — 570	
			31st 29 — 588 17 — 557	
			6 o/rs admitted to hospital sick during month. 13 o/rs demobilised in December '18 do do do January '19 5 officers & 193 o/rs do do	

J.R.Wood Capt
a/Adjt for Lieut Colonel
Commanding 15th (SUFFOLK) Bn
THE SUFFOLK REGIMENT

SUY.2 93

HQ 230 Inf Bde.

Herewith War Diary for
the month of February 1919.

1-3-19   H P Wood Capt
                    adjt
           for _____ Lieut. Colonel
        Commanding 15th (Suffolk Yeomanry) Bn.
              THE SUFFOLK REGIMENT

Army Form C. 2118.

WAR DIARY
or
INTELLIGENCE SUMMARY.
(Erase heading not required.)

15th Yeo Bn. Suffolk Regt.

Place	Date	Hour	Summary of Events and Information	Remarks and references to Appendices
HERINNES ref: map BELGIUM Sheet 38 1/40,000 and BRUSSELS 1/100,000	February 1-7		Hard frosty weather prevailed and the hours (daily) military Training consisted chiefly Physical Training & short marches. Educational Training as previously. On 7th inst. an order was received to prepare a draft of 10 Officers and 200 OR's (under command of Major 3rd Army Order XIV of January 19) for despatch to 2nd Bn. Suffolks 2nd Army.	
	7-14		Snow and frosty weather still continued. Military and Educational Training as previously. Recreational Training, games etc were not practicable owing to weather.	
	14-21		Training as for previous week. Frost began to give about the 15th inst. The Bn used the hot baths at VOLLEZEEL on Sunday 16th inst. A change of under clothing available.	
	21-23		The draft for 2nd Suffolks had been organised as a company and concentrated in Hillock, and owing to extensive demobilisation the remainder of the Bn was organised as another company. Orders received that the Bn in conjunction with Bde Group would move on the 25th to billet in GRAMMONT. The reason for this was to concentrate the Bde & Divn more, some units being very scattered.	

Army Form C. 2118.

WAR DIARY
or
INTELLIGENCE SUMMARY.
(Erase heading not required.) 15th Yeo Bn Suffolk Regt.

Instructions regarding War Diaries and Intelligence Summaries are contained in F. S. Regs., Part II. and the Staff Manual respectively. Title pages will be prepared in manuscript.

Place	Date	Hour	Summary of Events and Information	Remarks and references to Appendices
HERINNES	February 24		Move to GRAMMONT postponed until 27th inst	
GRAMMONT	27.		The Bn marched out from HERINNES at 0930 and arrived to billet in GRAMMONT at 1245	
	28.		Inspection of billet by CO; troops company exercised in guards and sentry drill.	

Effective Strength (from A.F. B.213.)

Feby	Offs	ORs
7th	28	643
14th	26	611
21	27	445
28	27	359

Return Strength

	Offs	ORs
7/2	17	534
14/2	21	515
21/2	18	399
28/2	15	290

Admitted sick to hospital during month - 1 officer and 16 O.R.

Numbers demobilised during month:-

Feb:	Offs.	ORs.	Feb.	Offs	ORs	Feb.	Offs	ORs
1st	1	6	12		1	23rd		22
2		9	13		14	24		46
6		6	14		2	27		3
7		13	15		3	28		8
9		26	16	1	61			
10th		1	20		67	Demob. whilst on leave 10		
			21		5			
			22			Total demob. } OFFS 2 ORS 302 for Feby.		

J.P. Word Capt & Adjt
Lieut. Colonel
Commanding 15th (Suffolk Yeomanry) Bn.
THE SUFFOLK REGIMENT

15th Bn Stafford Regt

WAR DIARY
or
INTELLIGENCE SUMMARY.
(Erase heading not required.)

Army Form C. 2118.

MARCH 1919

Place	Date	Hour	Summary of Events and Information	Remarks and references to Appendices
GRAMMONT	March 1		The Bn remained in billets in Grammont with Demobilisation proceeding. The draft of 196 men for the Army of Occupation still left in reserves but Kosher orders have been received about them. They paraded daily under OC Coy for rifle drill + guard duties. Arms Bln different in filing grounds + in state when obtainable to help training is being carried out.	
	12th		Orders have been received that Lt Col T. de la G. Grissell Comdg proceed to UK for Demobilisation, handing over temporary Command to A.P. Baker. A board was assembled to check the stores + equipment of the Bn. Important A/c + nominal Rolls of Bn adminstuchs by the Bn. which were found correct duly handed over.	
	15th		Lt Col T. de la G. Grissell, M.C. proceeds to UK	
	16.		Brigadier General D.A. Kennedy CMG pzzee who had Commanded the 23rd Brigade since July 1918 proceeds UK on attachm...	

Army Form C. 2118.

WAR DIARY
or
INTELLIGENCE SUMMARY.
(Erase heading not required.)

Instructions regarding War Diaries and Intelligence Summaries are contained in F. S. Regs., Part II. and the Staff Manual respectively. Title pages will be prepared in manuscript.

Place	Date	Hour	Summary of Events and Information	Remarks and references to Appendices
	March		Commenced in the 3rd Northern Div.	
GRANTHAM	16th		Order rec'd for the following volunteer officers transferred up to No Army of Occupation from 1st/2nd Bn Alex Ralph Regt positions: Lts Gill, Morris, Hale, Hanley & Powell. That named being replaced with W.K.	
	20th		Orders received for 145 ORs & 1 volunteer officer. Known OR in 1st/2nd Bn Alex Suffolk Regt on the 22nd. Lt Stallman (detach'd Yeo.) proceeds in charge accompanied by 2 Lt Knittle of the Batt's Knittle proceeds at 18.30 when 22 OR's went at the Station to parade ground & entrained at ENTRAIN at 22.00 same date.	
	21st		The balance of the draft consisting of 23 ORs under Lt RUTTER proceeds to 1st/2nd Bn Suffolk Regt.	
	22.22		A/GHQ has now rec'd that - all movements of troops for demobilization + leave have been stopped owing to the serious position of the strikes in England.	
	24th		The steps has been cancelled & demobilization & leave resumed normal lines.	

WAR DIARY
or
INTELLIGENCE SUMMARY.
(Erase heading not required.)

Army Form C. 2118.

Place	Date	Hour	Summary of Events and Information	Remarks and references to Appendices
ARMENT	25		Our Divisional inter football team competition was started	
			The first drawing 11 Batts meeting 114 were defeated in the first round	
	30		Lt W Murray proceeded to England for Demobilisation	
			Ration Strength of Bn during the month of March has been:—	
			March 1st 18 officers 285 ORs	
			„ 8th 19 „ 278 „	
			„ 15th 18 „ 251 „	
			„ 22nd 13 „ 106 „	
			„ 29th 12 „ 58 „	
				A Robins Capt for wfs
				Comdg 10th M.G Bn
				Suffolk Regt

Army Form C. 2118.

WAR DIARY
or
INTELLIGENCE SUMMARY.
(Erase heading not required.) 15th Yeo Bn Suffolk Regt.

Instructions regarding War Diaries and Intelligence Summaries are contained in F. S. Regs., Part II. and the Staff Manual respectively. Title pages will be prepared in manuscript.

Place	Date	Hour	Summary of Events and Information	Remarks and references to Appendices
	April 1919.			
GRAMMONT Belgium. (ref map Belgium Sheet 30. 1/40,000)	1		During the month of April the Bn remained in billets in Grammont, the Effective strength at this date was 19 officers and 87 ors. Demobilisation of those eligible and surplus to cadre proceeded slowly throughout the month leaving at the end of the month an effective strength of 9 officers 60 ors	
V.2.b.	4		The Ordnance inspecting staff visited the Bn and inspected the stores and accounts relating thereto. The stores at this date were nearing completion to the establishment required on the Mobilisation Store Table. The inspecting officer was satisfied and endorsed the accounts.	
	10.		2 ors (retainable under A.O.55) were despatched for duty with the Chinese Depot at NOYELLES	
	15.		24 officers and 4 ors (retainable under A.O.55) were despatched for duty with No. 122 Prisoner of War Company 5th Area	
	24.		One OR (retainable) despatched to 4th Suffolks, to which unit the Bn had already sent 6 officers and 168 ors	12 r

(A9175) Wt W2358/F360 600,000 12/17 D. D. & L. Sch 5B Forms/C2118/15

Army Form C. 2118.

WAR DIARY
or
INTELLIGENCE SUMMARY.
(Erase heading not required.)

Place	Date	Hour	Summary of Events and Information	Remarks and references to Appendices
GRAMMONT	April 25		The 5 remaining animals (mules) were sent to III Corps Concentration Camp for disposal. These mules have previously been classified Group X. 64 for the army. Emergency rations were drawn in future by hand carts borrowed from the civilians. Two days rations being drawn on alternate days. No military training was carried out during this month owing to the reduced strength of the Bn. Men available for duty were daily employed on guards, working parties, packing & preparing stores for subsequent entrainment and embarkation, cleaning the 36 Lewis guns and equipment. Outdoor & games were organised within the Brigade. What drives and dances were held weekly to provide amusement for the evenings. Some difficulty was experienced in obtaining recreation grounds from the civilians and as an alternative to the shortage of playing fields the division provided lorries at intervals for free trips to various	

Army Form C. 2118.

WAR DIARY
or
INTELLIGENCE SUMMARY.
(Erase heading not required.) 13ᵗʰ Ber. Bn. Suffolk Regt.

Place	Date May	Hour	Summary of Events and Information	Remarks and references to Appendices
GRAMMONT. Belgium (ref map TOURNAI 1/100,000) 3.K. 5525.			The cadre of the battalion remained billeted in GRAMMONT for the month.	
	4		Four ORs proceeded on leave to OSTEND for 2 days by lorry provided by Division for free trips to places of interest in Belgium.	
	5		Orders were received that the cadre establishment of Inf. Bns. would be reduced to 3 offrs + 36 ors + that the releasable personnel which would become surplus (i.e. 1 offr + 10 ors) would be sent for dispersal as soon as possible.	
	6		One ort (intemabile under A.O. 55. 1919) returned from hospital was despatched to join the 4ᵗʰ Bn Suffolks Army of the Rhine. Lieut D.C. WADDELL (I.W.T. attd) proceeded for demobilization, independent route.	
	7		Four ORs proceeded for 2 days leave at OSTEND by lorry.	
	9		Nine ors, releasable on reduction of Cadre, proceeded for demobilization at 0200, by lorry, which conveyed them to railhead at GHISLENGHIEN Stn. The 10ᵗʰ ort was admitted to hospital	

Army Form C. 2118.

WAR DIARY
or
INTELLIGENCE SUMMARY.
(Erase heading not required.)

Instructions regarding War Diaries and Intelligence Summaries are contained in F. S. Regs., Part II. and the Staff Manual respectively. Title pages will be prepared in manuscript.

Place	Date	Hour	Summary of Events and Information	Remarks and references to Appendices
	April			
GROTHART			Places of interest in Belgium. Places visited were Waterloo, Ghent, Ostend, Brussels. Following is list showing demobilisation during this month:—	
			OFFRS ORS	
			3rd April 2	
			9 " 4	
			10 " 1	
			14 " 3	
			21 " 1	
			25 " 1	
			Effective Strengths Ration Strengths	
			OFFRS OR OFFRS OR	
	5th April		19 87 10 57	
	12 "		12 78 7 54	
	19 "		11 67 6 49	
	26 "		9 60 3 42	

N.O. Wood Captn & Maj or
Commanding 15th (Suffolk Yeomanry) Bn.
THE SUFFOLK REGIMENT

Army Form C. 2118.

WAR DIARY
or
INTELLIGENCE SUMMARY.
(Erase heading not required.) 15th Yeo. Cov. Suffolk Regt.

Place	Date May	Hour	Summary of Events and Information	Remarks and references to Appendices
GRAMMONT	9		Two ORs proceeded on 2 days leave to OSTEND by lorry	
	12		A cricket match was played between teams of the 230 Inf Bde Cadres and the 242 Army Bde RFA Cadres. The former team won by 11 runs. The umpires were supplied by the Artillery	
	13.		Capt A ROSLING (Suff (K gun) attd, proceeded for demobilisation, independent route.	
	16.		Return of cricket match played on 12th inst. 230 Inf Bde won	
	20.		The Bn Stores & equipment were moved to another storehouse nearer the railway stn, where entrainment would eventually take place.	
	21st		Loading the Bn stores & equipment into the waggons & limbers, numbering & marking. Artillery equipment & vehicles ready for entrainment. Stores & equipment were now made up as required by the amended Mobilization Store Table for transference to UK. The new storehouse was large enough to accomodate the whole of the Bn transport with stores loaded. There	

Army Form C. 2118.

WAR DIARY
or
INTELLIGENCE SUMMARY.
(Erase heading not required.) 15th Yeo. Bn. Suffolk Regt.

Place	Date	Hour	Summary of Events and Information	Remarks and references to Appendices
GRAMMONT	21.6.22.		was about a ton of stores which could not be loaded into the vehicles and for which lorry arrangements were being made.	
	23.		4 O.R.s lorry trip to OSTEND	
	31.		Orders received that a further reduction would be made in all Cadre establishments by 75% of the original establishment (i.e. 4 Offrs & 46 O.R.s Inf. Bns. to be reduced to approximately 2 Offrs & 12 O.R.s. All Cadres thus reduced would be collected round railheads so that the personnel could be pooled for guarding equipment etc. Instructions would follow as to disposal of the personnel thus made available for immediate demobilisation.	
			10. O.R.s proceeded on U.K. leave during the month. Vacancies for local leave were generous. The weather was exceptionally fine throughout the month.	

Weekly Strength (Bn H.Q. B 2 & 3)

Date	Effective Offrs	O.Rs	Ration Offrs	O.Rs
3rd	3	62	6	41
10th	7	50	5	28
17th	6	39	4	30
24th	6	38	4	27
31st	5	38	3	27

W.W.Wood Capt
Commanding 15th (Suffolk Yeomanry) Bn.
THE SUFFOLK REGIMENT

D.AAG a.

Passed

Major
i/c No. 1 Sub-Section Record Office
H.Q., British Troops in France & Flanders

Army Form C. 2118.

WAR DIARY
or
INTELLIGENCE SUMMARY.
(Erase heading not required.) 15th Yeo: Bn Suffolk Regt.

Place	Date	Hour	Summary of Events and Information	Remarks and references to Appendices
GRAMMONT. Belgium (Ref map TOURNAI. 1/100,000 3.K.55.25)	June 5th		Orders received for reconstruction of Cadres into "Equipment Guard" + Cadre. Equip. Guard of 2 Off/s (Capt. H.P. Wood, Capt. & Q. TUTTLE) & 12 O.Rs. Cadre of remainder. O.C. Equipment Guard to take over all responsibility for stores & Equipment other than those belonging to the Regt. privately	
	10th 11th		Repacking Stores according to orders	
	13th		Audit Board assembled by order of C.O. to check all Stores Equipment & accounts prior to demobilisation	
	15th		Orders received that all stores & cleaning-stone-will be sent to AINTREE Packages branded accordingly by	

WAR DIARY
or
INTELLIGENCE SUMMARY

Army Form C. 2118.

1st Yeo. Batt. Suffolk Regt.

Place	Date	Hour	Summary of Events and Information	Remarks and references to Appendices
GRAMMONT Belgium	June 17.		Capt. W.C. Halsey proceeds on demob. in charge of Cadre of 10th The Buffs as they have no officer.	YB ## / 3 Cadre
TOURNAI 1/100,000				
3K 35.25	19	10.30	Cadre under Major G.P. Barker & 19 ORs. Leave GRAMMONT	
		20.00	Arrive Demob. Camp LILLE.	
	20.	21.08	Leave LILLE for BOULOGNE.	
	21.		Stay sid. in siding entered BOULOGNE 8.00 - 20.00	
		21.08	Arrive TERLINGTHUN CAMP BOULOGNE	
	22.	8.00	Men's clothes disinfected	
		10.00	March to MALBOROUGH CAMP BOULOGNE	
	24.	16.00	Parade for embarcation on S.S. BIARRITZ	

G.P.B. under
G.P. Barker Major
Suffolk Yeo.

www.ingramcontent.com/pod-product-compliance
Lightning Source LLC
Chambersburg PA
CBHW081450160426

43193CB00013B/2438